OSCAR,
CAT-ABOUT-TOWN

James Herriot

Illustrated by Ruth Brown

Michael Joseph – London

I looked at the stray cat which a kind little girl had brought to my surgery. He was very pretty with stripes of auburn, gold and grey, but he looked terribly thin and ill.

The little girl said that nobody knew where the cat had come from, so she left him with me.

With my wife Helen by my side I examined him thoroughly and found that he was suffering from starvation. But the strange thing was that he purred loudly all the time.

'He's so weak that he can hardly stand, but he's purring,' I said. 'You can see he's a good-natured cat.'

For a few days Helen gave him beef broth and milk to make him strong and when he walked into the kitchen to eat some of Sam's dinner of meat and biscuits, we knew he was well again.

'We shall call him Oscar,' Helen said.

'You mean you want to keep him?'

'Yes, he's a lovely, friendly cat, and so pretty, and since we don't know who owns him, he must stay with us. He and Sam seem to get along so well.' Oscar purred his approval and his big purr became part of our lives.

Oscar had been with us for several weeks when I came
home and found Helen looking very worried. 'It's
Oscar. He's gone!' she said.

'What do you mean?'

'I think he's run away.'

I became worried too because I knew he had run away
from somewhere before we found him and it made me sad
to think that we might be going to lose our cat after we had
grown so fond of him.

In the darkness, Helen and I searched all over the garden
and the lane behind the house. Then, although it had begun
to rain heavily, we began to explore the streets and side-
alleys of the little town of Darrowby. After two hours we
could not find him and Helen had tears in her eyes.

'I think we'd better go home, Jim,' she said. 'He's gone, I
know he has.'

On our way home, we passed the brightly-lit window of the Women's Institute Hall. I stopped suddenly. 'I think I can see Oscar in there!' I cried. We both peered in through the window and to our delight we could see our cat among the ladies.

We ran inside. There was a hat-making competition in progress. Various ladies were lined up, wearing some very original and pretty hats. Oscar was walking along with the judge, listening to her comments and examining each hat as though he himself were an expert. Sometimes he jumped up in the air to have a closer look.

When we were able to reach Oscar he was delighted to see us and purred and rubbed round our legs. One of the ladies said that he had been there for the whole evening and had seemed to enjoy himself thoroughly.

It was lovely to have him back – but one afternoon a week later, he disappeared again. Helen and I looked everywhere and again we were just giving up hope when we heard two women speaking as they came out of Darrowby's Town Hall.

'Did you see that funny cat in there?' one of them said, laughing. 'I've never seen one like him.'

Helen and I looked at each other, then hurried into the hall where a jumble sale was taking place. And there was Oscar right in the thick of things.

He was stepping daintily along the display tables, inspecting the old shoes, books, pictures, ornaments, crockery, and he looked really happy. Now and then he cocked his head on one side when something caught his fancy. Once more it was clear that he was enjoying every moment and we didn't want to disturb him, but the sale was soon over and he greeted us with joy.

When he went missing again on the following Saturday we were not so worried because we knew he would be at some gathering.

'Darrowby School is playing Wickley School at football today,' Helen said.

We rushed round to the football field and, as we expected, Oscar was there among the spectators, running along the line, following the ball, jumping up and down at the cheering. We let him enjoy himself for a while before bringing him home, and then we had a chat by the fireside.

'Now we know,' said Helen.

I nodded. 'Yes, when he disappears, he isn't running away at all. He's just visiting. He likes getting around, he loves people, especially in groups, and he's interested in what they do. He's a natural mixer.'

Helen looked down at our cat. 'Of course, that's it . . . he's a socialite!'

'Exactly, a high-stepper!'

'A swinger!'

'A cat-about-town!'

We both laughed, not only because it was a funny idea but because we were relieved that Oscar wasn't going to run away after all. Oscar seemed to be laughing, too, as he looked up at us, adding his loud, throbbing purr to the merriment.

We were all happy and everything seemed to be perfect – but a few days later we received an unexpected blow.

I was finishing the evening surgery. I looked round the door of the waiting room and saw only a man and two little red-headed boys. Helen came in and began to tidy the magazines on the table.

The man had the rough, weathered face of a farmer and he twirled a cloth cap nervously in his hands.

'Mr Herriot,' he said, 'my name is Sep Gibbons and I think you've got my cat.'

'What makes you think that?' I asked in surprise.

'Well, when we moved from Darrowby to Wickley, the cat went missing. We thought he might be trying to find his way back to his old home. We hunted everywhere, but we couldn't find him. My boys were broken-hearted. They loved that cat.'

'But why do you think we've got him?'

'Well, my boys were playing football here last week and they are sure they spotted him watching the game. He always liked to be with people, go to meetings and social events. So I just had to come and find out.'

'This cat you lost,' I asked, 'what did he look like?'

'Sort of tabby but with gingery stripes. He was right bonny.'

My heart thumped.

That sounded very like Oscar.

I could see that Helen was worried, too. 'Just a moment,' she said. 'Oscar's in the kitchen. I'll bring him through.'

When she returned with the cat in her arms, the little boys called out, 'Tiger! Oh, Tiger, Tiger!'

'That's our cat, all right,' said Mr Gibbons. 'And doesn't he look well! The boys called him Tiger because of his gingery stripes.'

He looked at the two boys flopped happily on the floor as Oscar, purring loudly with delight, rolled around them. 'The boys used to play with him like that for hours. They cried a lot when we lost him.'

'Well, Mr Gibbons,' said Helen with a catch in her voice, 'you'd better take him. He was your cat first, and you searched for him so hard, and I can see that the boys love him.'

'Well, that's very kind of you. Please come and see him whenever you like. Wickley is only twenty miles away.' He picked up Oscar and left.

We missed Oscar terribly, but we knew we had done the right thing. He really belonged to the Gibbons family who loved him and would be kind to him.

One afternoon we were out shopping in the nearby town, and I looked at my watch. 'It's only five o'clock. Why don't we go and see Oscar at Wickley, it's not far from here.'

The Gibbons' cottage was at the far end of Wickley village and when Mrs Gibbons opened the door to us she didn't know who we were, but when she heard the name Herriot, she was delighted to see us.

'Come in and have a cup of tea,' she said.

We went inside and were greeted by Sep and the boys. As Mrs Gibbons busied herself with the kettle, we looked eagerly around the room for Oscar and within a few moments he trotted in. He took one look at Helen, then jumped onto her lap, and rubbed his face against her hand.

'He knows me, he knows me!' Helen cried in delight.

'Yes,' Sep said. 'You were kind to him and he'll never forget you, and we won't either.'

I tickled the cat's cheek as he lay curled happily on Helen's lap. However, after about half an hour he gave her a final rub and purr then jumped down and trotted from the room into the back garden.

Mrs Gibbons laughed. 'He still goes visiting. Let's see, Thursday, isn't it? That's when he goes to the brass band practice at the village hall. It's just next door and he slips through a hole in the hedge.'

'Oh, let's go and see him!' Helen said.

'We'll pop round there when we've finished our tea,' said Mrs Gibbons.

In the village hall, we all stood in a row and watched Oscar moving among the band players, jumping in delight at each boom from the drum, creeping close to the slide of the trombone which seemed to fascinate him.

'There's Oscar!' I said. 'There's Tiger!' said one of the boys, and we all laughed.

'It doesn't matter what we call him,' said Sep. 'He belongs to all of us now.'

In the same series by James Herriot
MOSES THE KITTEN
ONLY ONE WOOF
THE CHRISTMAS DAY KITTEN
BONNY'S BIG DAY
BLOSSOM COMES HOME
THE MARKET SQUARE DOG

MICHAEL JOSEPH LTD

Published by the Penguin Group
27 Wrights Lane, London W8 5TZ, England
Viking Penguin, a division of Penguin Books USA Inc, 375 Hudson Street, New York, New York, 10014
Penguin Books Australia Ltd, Ringwood, Victoria, Australia
Penguin Books Canada Ltd, 2801 John Street, Markham, Ontario, Canada L3R 1B4
Penguin Books (NZ) Ltd, 182–190 Wairau Road, Auckland 10, New Zealand
Penguin Books Ltd, Registered Offices: Harmondsworth, Middlesex, England

First published 1990

Copyright © 1977, 1990 by James Herriot
Copyright © illustrations 1990 by Ruth Brown

Typeset in linotron 14/18pt Garamond Light ITC by Goodfellow and Egan, Cambridge
Colour reproduction by Anglia Graphics, Bedford
Printed and bound in Italy by Arnoldo Mondadori, Verona

A CIP catalogue record of this book is available from the British Library

ISBN 0 7181 3448 6

The moral right of the author has been asserted